Oakville Ontario in Photos, Saving Our History One Photo at a Time

Photography
by Barbara Raué
2012

Series Name:
Cruising Ontario

Book 4: Oakville

Cover Photo: 1856 Custom House and Bank of Toronto on the Erchless Estate – now part of Oakville Museum

Oakville is situated on Lake Ontario in southern Ontario. In 1793, Dundas Street was surveyed for a military road. By 1807, British immigrants settled the area around Dundas Street and on the shores of Lake Ontario. In 1827, William Chisholm purchased 960 acres of uncleared land at the mouth of Sixteen Mile Creek. He built mills, and laid out the Town of Oakville and opened the harbour to shipping. The area was developed by his son, Robert Kerr Chisholm and his brother-in-law Thomas Merrick. Oakville's first industries included shipbuilding, timber shipment, and wheat farming. The town became industrialized with the opening of oil refineries, and Procor (manufactured railway shipping cars), and the establishment of the Ford Motor Company's Canadian headquarters and plant.

46 Burnet Street

52 Burnet Street

77 Burnet Street

75 Burnet Street

67 Burnet Street

43 Burnet Street

38 Burnet Street – 1855 – Michael Quinn, Shoemaker

37 Burnet Street

76 Chisholm Street

63 Chisholm Street

60 Chisholm Street

54 Chisholm Street

52 Chisholm Street

45 Chisholm Street

48 Chisholm Street

44 Chisholm Street

40 Chisholm Street

37 Chisholm Street

#11

#39

#59

50 Forsythe Street

Oakville Museum

Erchless
1858 – Robert Kerr Chisholm

Thomas House – 1829
The original home of the Merrick Thomas Family

Oakville's First Post Office – 1835-1857

21 Thomas Street at corner of Front Street

174 Front Street – 1837
James McDonald, Carpenter

1852 – Duncan Chisholm, Shipbuilder

1852 – Duncan Chisholm, Shipbuilder

1839 – Captain William Wilson
1854 – "Glenorchy" – Peter MacDougald, Grain Merchant,
Mayor of Oakville 1875

1839 – P. A. MacDougald

St. Jude's Anglican Church

St. Jude's Anglican Church
Founded in 1839, built from 1883
160 William Street

1834 – Thomas and John Sweeney, Ship Carpenters

1835 – Edward Anderson, Mariner

1833 –The Summer House

1850 – Captain Samuel McGiffin, Master Mariner

1875 – George K Chisholm, General Retail Store
64 Navy Street

1855 – Jeremiah Hagman, Carriage Maker
68 Navy Street

1828 – Ship's Chandlery established by William Chisholm, Oakville's Founder – 115 Navy Street
1891 – Captain James Andrew, Yacht Builder

45 Navy Street

1830 Captain William Wilson, married
Moved to this site in 1859

1833 – Captain Robert Wilson, Mariner

1838 – John Moore, Mariner
1853 – The Frontier House

1835 – David Patterson, Shipbuilder
#19

212 Front Street

43 Dunn Street

Knox Presbyterian Church
89 Dunn Street at Lakeshore Road

1838 – Justus W. Williams, General Merchant

Downtown

Corner of Dunn and Church Streets

235 Randall Street

St. John's United Church
Established 1832 with Justus Wright Williams in attendance
262 Randall Street – brick building built 1877

Sheridan College

Circa 1849 – Captain William Wilson
Circa 1894 – Francis Matthews, Soda Water Works

Circa 1870 – Captain Wilson

MacLachlan College

1816 – oldest house in Halton Region
Amos Biggar, United Empire Loyalist
Original Location: 502 Dundas Street West
Classic Revival style
Now The Cork House 2441 Neyagawa Boulevard

Wooden ceiling beams from the original construction

Knox Sixteen Presbyterian Church

Knox Sixteen Presbyterian Church
First Service held 1844
Church constructed 1846
Brick exterior added 1899

Modern buildings

www.ingramcontent.com/pod-product-compliance
Lightning Source LLC
Chambersburg PA
CBHW061520180526
45171CB00001B/261